THE BLUE ROSE

To Jackie —
because you care and
understand.
        Love
        Jerora.

THE
BLUE ROSE

by
GERDA KLEIN

with photographs by

NORMA HOLT

LAWRENCE HILL and COMPANY

New York · Westport

*This book is dedicated
to
Jenny Innerfield
with love.*
G. W. K.

We are deeply indebted to the

KENNEDY CHILD STUDY CENTER, New York
and to Mrs. Anne Hooper
for their cooperation.

THE BLUE ROSE

Jenny.

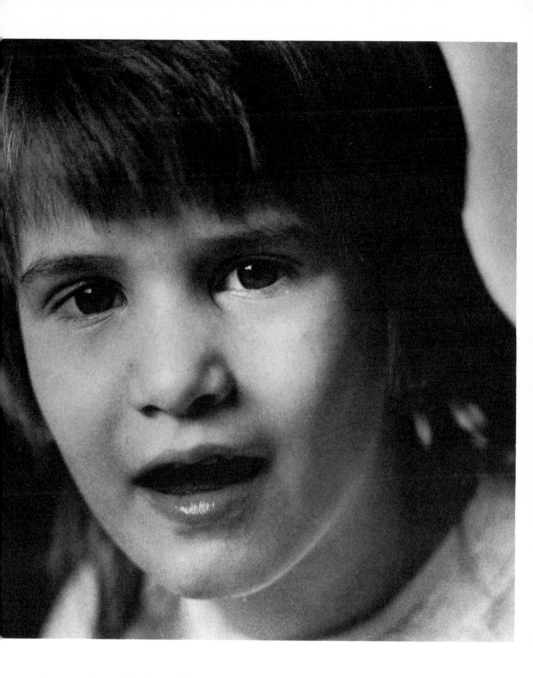

Jenny is a little girl—a lovely little girl.
She has brown eyes and dark brown hair.

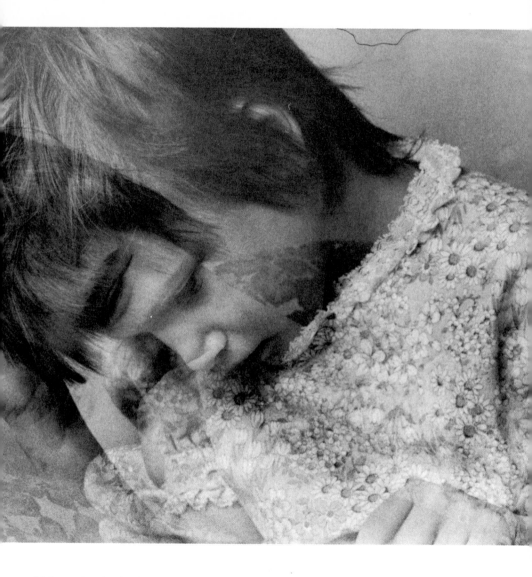

If her hair falls into her eyes
she brushes it away, but – – – –

her hand does not go straight to her forehead.

Instead it curves around like
a flower first opening its petals.
Then she brushes her hair out of her eyes.

She looks up at you and smiles.
Her nose wrinkles, her lips curve up at the corners,
she says, "Hi.—Hi Jenny."
She repeats, "Hi, hi, hi."

Sometimes she goes into an awkward little dance.

You see, Jenny is different.
Different?
Yes, different from most other little girls.

But surely all people don't have to be alike,
think alike,
act alike
or look alike.

To me, Jenny is like a blue rose.

A *blue* rose?

Have you ever seen a blue rose?
There are white roses
and pink roses
and yellow roses,
and of course lots of red roses.
But blue?

Every gardener would love to raise a blue rose.
People would come from afar to see it.
It is rare and different and beautiful.
Jenny is different, too,
and so, in a way,
she is like a blue rose.

This is the story of Jenny.
We know her well. She is our friend.
Jenny was born on the 4th of July.

What fun!

She likes to be told over and over
about the day she was born.
It was a summer day,
not a cloud in the blue sky.
A day warm and golden with sunshine.

Jenny's father was at the hospital with her mother, and Jenny's big sister went with us.
What a lucky little girl Jenny is, we often say, to be born on the 4th of July.

Her birthday will always be a national holiday.

We often talk of the years ahead.
Jenny growing up,
learning to walk,
to talk.
Jenny going to school,

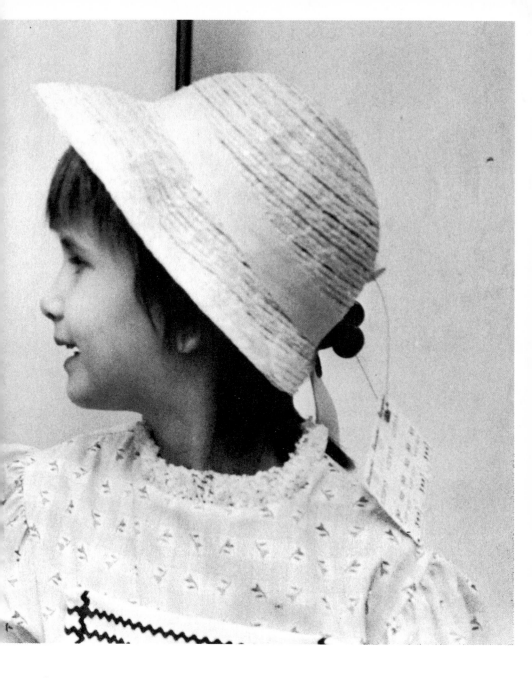

Jenny on a day far, far away
being a grownup young lady . . .
and getting married.

Jenny's sister and our children were very excited
by the idea that they would be able to say,
"We remember the day when Jenny was born."

And then Jenny came home from the hospital.
A pink baby, all cuddly and round.
At the beginning Jenny cried very often.
She cried more than most babies.

Why?

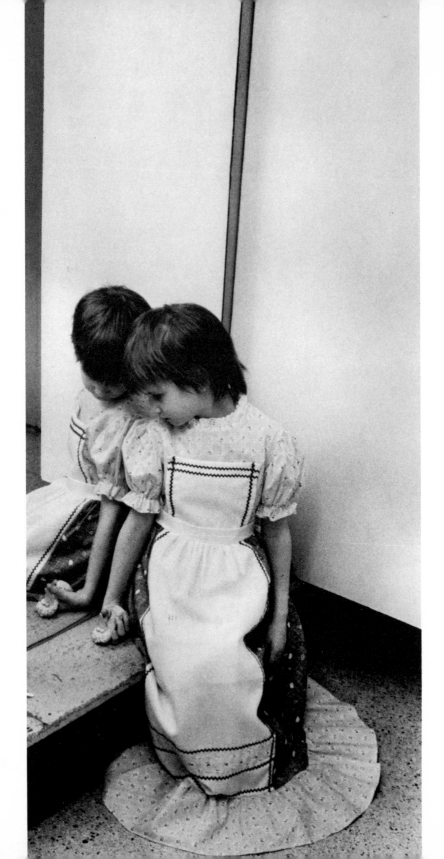

Well, perhaps
she saw different shadows that frightened her.
Perhaps she heard sounds that were strange to her.
When she was older,
Jenny always stayed close to her mother and
held on to her tightly.

You know, when a kitten loses its tail,
it is said to gain sharper ears.
It's true that a tail helps a kitten run faster.
But a kitten without a tail hears better
and can detect approaching footsteps
long before other kittens do.

Some people don't know
about such a kitten's fine ears;
they only see the lack of a tail.

Some children are cruel and stare and taunt:
The kitten has no tail,
the kitten has no tail!

Sometimes Jenny would run up to her mother
and clutch her tightly.
For no apparent reason at all.
At least, for none that we could see.

Jenny often worried.

And so we came to understand that Jenny's world
was a little different,
unknown to us, in some ways.
We began to think that she was in a world
in which *we* might not feel completely at home.
To go there might, in a way,
be like going to another planet.

Remember when we watched our astronauts
landing on the moon?
How carefully they stepped onto the surface,
slowly testing the ground they did not know.
If there had been moon people watching our men,
they might not have understood the fears
our men had of the unknown world.
Because it is *their* world,
they feel at home in it and know it well.
Our astronauts are great heroes to us.
We know that they are very handsome men and
we marvel at how easily they leaped
around on the moon and in space.
To the creatures of the moon
they might look quite different.

Moon people might think our men clumsy and ugly.

So, too, maybe Jenny sees things
with different eyes.
Maybe, also, she hears a different drummer.
In a way, it's as if Jenny is standing behind a screen,
a screen we cannot see.
Maybe it has beautiful colors such as we never see.
Maybe the colors distract Jenny at times
from paying attention when we talk to her.
Perhaps she listens to music we cannot hear.
It is said that fish have a language
and a music of their own—
a language and music, carried by the waves.
Music we cannot hear because
our ears are not fine enough.

So Jenny might hear sounds we never hear.
Maybe that is why she jumps up at times
and goes into her awkward dance.

I sometimes think Jenny is like a bird,
a bird with very short wings.
For such a bird, flying is very hard:
it takes more strength, more effort, more time.

A bird with normal wings takes flying for granted,
but the bird with short wings
has to work much harder at learning,
and in a way, it has to be smarter.

For Jenny to learn things to say and to read
or even to tie a bow, is very difficult.

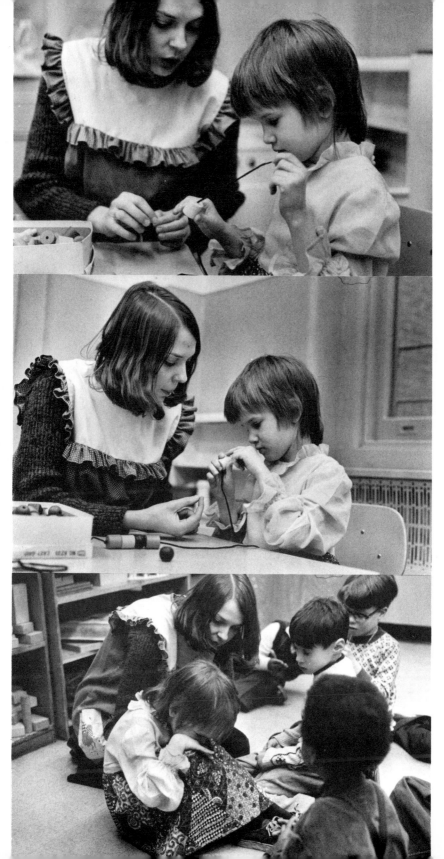

And so therefore,
we have to understand
how much she has accomplished
when she does learn something.

But there is another Jenny.
A Jenny who on a stormy winter afternoon
sits in her little rocking chair alone and rocks,
holding her doll in her arms.
She is very troubled
and puzzled

and she says slowly

"Mommy,
Sally says I'm retarded.
What does that mean, Mommy?
Retarded.
The children say retarded, and laugh.

Why?"

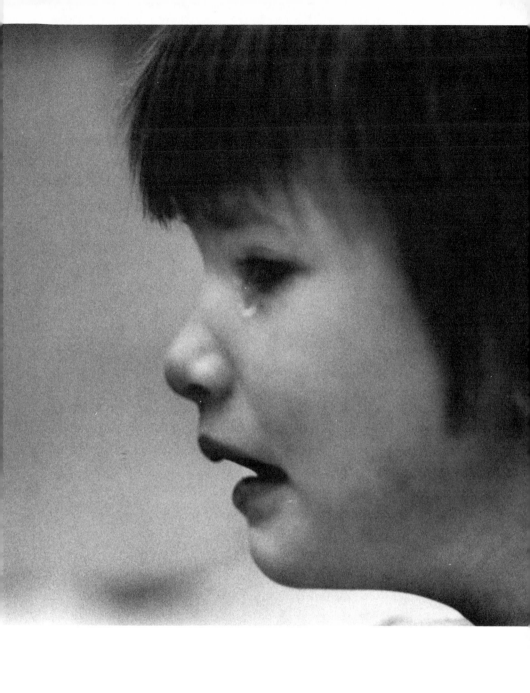

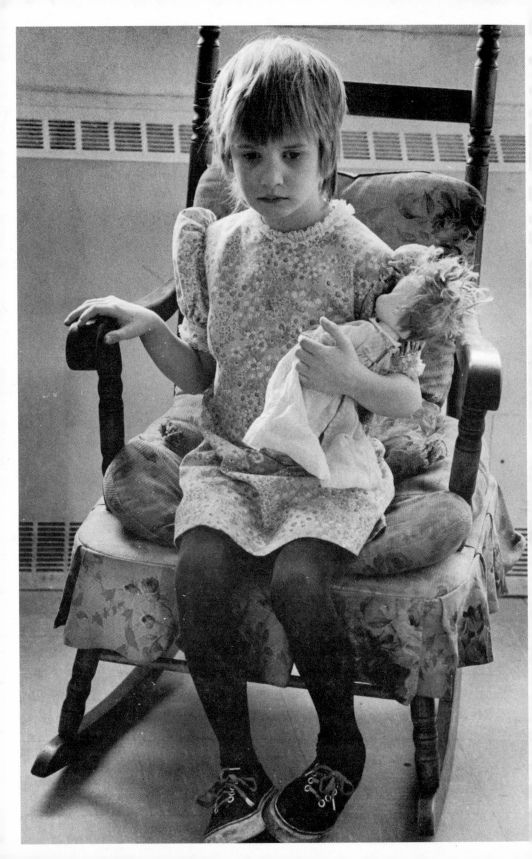

And Jenny rocks in her chair
and her eyes look like stars in the twilight.

There are many things Jenny does not understand.

And there are many things
other people don't understand about Jenny—
that Jenny is like a kitten without a tail,
that Jenny hears different music,
that she is like a bird with shorter wings
and has to be protected.

Jenny is like a blue rose, delicate and lovely.
And because there are so few blue roses,
we don't know much about them.

We only know
that they have to be tended more carefully
and *loved* more.